Who eats *who* in the Rainforest?

Robert Snedden

FRANKLIN WATTS
LONDON•SYDNEY

Designer: Cali Roberts
Editor: Constance Novis
Art Director: Peter Scoulding
Editor-in-Chief: John C. Miles
Picture Research: Diana Morris
Artwork: Ian Thompson

First published in 2005
by Franklin Watts
96 Leonard Street
London
EC2A 4XD

Franklin Watts Australia
45-51 Huntley Street
Alexandria
NSW 2015

ISBN 0 7496 6078 3

A CIP catalogue record for this book is
available from the British Library.

Printed in Times Offset Malaysia

Dewey classification number: 577.34

PICTURE CREDITS

Andrew Brown/Ecoscene: 18tr
John Cancalosi/Still Pictures: 5, 22
Stephen Coyne/Ecoscene: 4
Ecoscene: 18bl
Romain Garrouste/Still Pictures: 10
Michael Gore/Ecoscene: 17
Simon Grove/Ecoscene: 13
Martin Harvey/Still Pictures: 8, 20, 24
Adrian Hepworth/NHPA: 23
David Hosking/FLPA: 27
Wayne Lawler/Ecoscene: 12
Luiz C. Marego/Still Pictures: 15b, 16, 25
Robert Pickett/Ecoscene: 19b, 26
Knell Sandved/Ecoscene: 14
Dr. Patricia Schulz/Still Pictures: 7
Hans Thomashoff/Still Pictures: front cover, 1
S. Tiwari/Ecoscene: 9,15t
Heinrich Van Den Berg/WWI/Still Pictures: 11
Alan Watson/WWI/Still Pictures: 21
David Woodfall/Still Pictures: 6

*Every attempt has been made to clear copyright.
Should there be any inadvertent omission please apply to
the publisher for rectification.*

Note to parents and teachers
Every effort has been made by the Publishers to ensure
that the websites in this book are suitable for children,
that they are of the highest educational value, and that
they contain no inappropriate or offensive material.
However, because of the nature of the Internet, it is
impossible to guarantee that the contents of these sites
will not be altered. We strongly advise that Internet
access is supervised by a responsible adult.

Contents

Food and energy

All organisms (living things) share certain basic needs. One of these is the need for a place to live where it can find everything necessary for survival. This place is known as a habitat.

Every living thing is adapted to life in its habitat. A whale's habitat can be as vast as the ocean, whereas a tadpole's habitat can be as tiny as a pool of water trapped in a flower.

Energy is essential

All organisms need energy to live; they get this from their food. Plants make their own food through a process called photosynthesis. They capture energy from sunlight and use it to make sugar from simple chemicals. This provides the plant with energy, fuelling new growth.

Photosynthesis factory: a tropical rainforest in Sri Lanka

A chain begins

Unlike plants, animals cannot make their own food. They have to find it within their habitat. Many animals eat plants. By doing so they ingest (take in) a share of the energy that the plants captured from the sun. Other animals eat these plant-eaters and so energy is passed along from one living thing to another. This forms a food chain, like the example on the right, joining plants and animals together.

figs

toucan

emerald boa

Ancient forests

Rainforests are the oldest forests in the world. Over millions of years the plants and animals living there have evolved different ways of feeding and avoiding being eaten. In the process, many food chain links have been forged between the forest organisms.

The toucan uses its huge beak to pluck fruit and small animals from rainforest trees.

First link

Plants are at the beginning of almost every food chain. Tropical rainforests provide the perfect habitat for plant growth, as conditions in a rainforest are warm and wet all the time. Rainforest trees shed old leaves and produce new ones all year round.

Yummy!

Two acres of rainforest might have more than 750 kinds of tree.

Primary producers

Trees and plants growing in a rainforest are known as primary producers because they make, or produce, their own food through photosynthesis. They capture energy from the sunlight and store it in their leaves, stalks and roots. This energy is available to all the other living things, such as the sloths and jaguars higher up the rainforest food chains.

Who Eats Who?

jaguar

This area of rainforest is part of Canaima National Park in Venezuela.

leaves

sloth

Magnified plant cells. Plants make their own food from sunlight, carbon dioxide and water.

How photosynthesis works

Plants use the energy of sunlight to join up carbon dioxide from the air and water from the soil. Using these two ingredients the plant makes glucose, a type of sugar. Along with minerals drawn from the soil, the plants use this to make new plant material.

Scientists estimate that every year, in every square metre of rainforest, plants produce more than two kilograms of new plant material. That's a lot of food!

Producer, and consumer

Some rainforest plants feature further along the food chain. The pitcher plant of South-east Asia grows up to 10 metres tall and has pitcher-shaped leaves. These contain a nectar that insects love to drink.

Insects drop in for a nectar snack but quickly find out they cannot escape up the slippery insides. The plant digests and gains nutrients from the insects, rather like taking a vitamin supplement!

Linking together

The next links in a food chain are the animals. They cannot make their own food and have to eat the food that is produced by plants, or by other animals that have eaten plants. For this reason, animals are called consumers.

This African mountain gorilla is a primary consumer.

Primary consumers

The first animals in the chain are the plant-eaters (or herbivores). They are known as primary consumers. The primary consumers of the rainforest range from tiny leaf-boring insects to big mountain gorillas. However, most primary consumers are insects.

An incredible number of insects live in rainforests. Scientists who study rainforests believe there may be as many as 30 million different kinds of insects living there.

Living larder

Only a very dim light reaches the rainforest floor, so plants grow poorly at ground level. This means there is not much to eat on the forest floor. For this reason many large primary consumers live high up in the trees. The trees aren't just home for these animals, but are also where they find their food supply.

Secondary consumers

Plant-eaters always have to be on the alert for other animals that might want to eat them. Animals that eat other animals are known as secondary consumers, or carnivores. In the rainforest these include insects, spiders, giant centipedes, reptiles, birds and big cats.

Changing places

Animals don't always occupy the same place in the food chain. For example, a bird might eat an insect that had been nibbling a leaf, or it might eat a spider that had eaten an insect. So the bird can be both a secondary consumer and a tertiary consumer.

We're in the chain!

More than 3,000 different types of fruit grow in the rainforest. Forest people eat about 2,000 of them.

Secondary consumers: two praying mantises eat a moth on a flower head.

Weaving the web

A food chain is a simple way of showing how one living thing eats another but it only tells part of the story. It is very rare that one type of plant is eaten by only one type of animal.

Adapt to survive

Usually animals eat, and are eaten by, different things and so are part of more than one food chain. An animal with a wide diet has a better chance of surviving because if one type of food source becomes scarce the animal can eat something else.

First link: rainforest trees

Forest web

A tree growing in the rainforest is a source of food for many different animals. Insects, birds and mammals all feed on the flowers, leaves and fruits of the tree. They, in turn, are eaten by spiders, snakes, birds of prey, cats and other hunters of the forest. So the tree is part of a number of different food chains.

When different food chains are put together they form what is called a food web. The food web shows the feeding relationships between plants and animals throughout the whole habitat.

Climbing the pyramid

How many animals are there at each link of the chains that make up the food web? If you draw this number as a diagram you get a food pyramid. Many plants support the plant-eaters and meat-eaters above them. This is a useful way to think about how food chains and webs work.

As you can see, it takes a lot of plants to provide enough energy to feed only a few plant-eaters. The plant-eaters then support an even smaller number of meat-eaters.

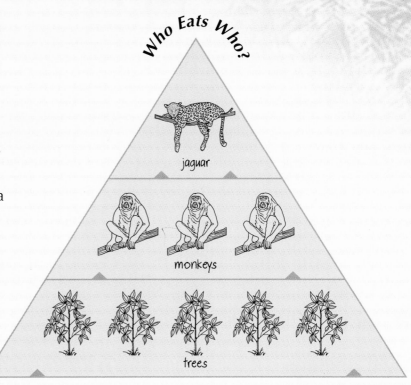

Who Eats Who?

jaguar

monkeys

trees

Losing energy

At every link a little energy is lost. Plants don't store all of the energy they capture from the sun. They need to use some of it to stay alive and to continue growing.

Plant-eaters almost never eat and digest whole plants, and meat-eaters almost never eat and digest whole plant-eaters. This means that some energy is lost at every link in the chain.

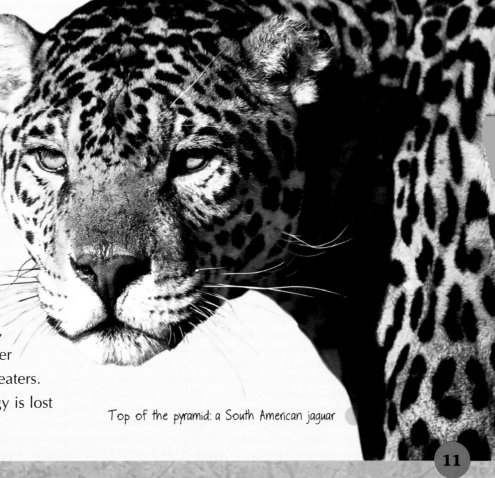

Top of the pyramid: a South American jaguar

11

Waste not, want not

Rainforests contain a greater abundance of life, and in greater numbers, than any other habitat in the world. You might think that is because rainforests grow on very fertile soils.

Nutrient loss

Rainforests actually grow on very poor soil. The high temperatures and heavy rainfall of the rainforest climate remove the nutrients from the soil much more quickly than in colder climates. So, what is the secret of rainforest growth?

Rainforest recycling

Leaves, animal droppings and other materials fall to the forest floor from the trees above. These are swiftly eaten by ants and other small animals. This is the first step in the rainforest recycling process.

Next, bacteria – microscopic organisms that thrive in the warmth of the rainforest – along with fungi that grow among the tree roots, break the material down even further. In this way the bacteria and fungi continue the decomposition process begun by the forest minibeasts.

Living things that get their energy from the waste material of others are called decomposers. They swiftly break down fallen leaves and other plant and animal remains. This releases the nutrients locked up in the remains and makes them available for the trees and other plants to use again.

These Australian termites help to break down rainforest plant material.

Unbroken chain

Without the work of the decomposers the rainforest soil would soon run out of nutrients. Trees, the primary producers of the rainforest, and the decomposers, which are the final link in the chain, need each other in order to survive.

The trees provide food for the bacteria and fungi in the form of falling leaves. The bacteria and fungi break the leaves down to provide the nutrients that new trees need in order to grow.

Web weaving

Birds and small mammals often eat the larger decomposers, such as ants and millipedes. So, the decomposers also find themselves at different points on the food chain. It's all part of the complex rainforest food web.

Who Eats Who?

leaves

insects

bird

tree

nutrients into soil

snake

decomposers (bacteria)

dead snake

Fungi, such as these, grow on the rainforest floor.

Treetop chains

If the rainforests are the world's richest habitat then most of the wealth of wildlife in the forest is found in the treetops. Around nine-tenths of the living things in the rainforest are found in the forest canopy, or overstorey.

Canopy cornucopia

The canopy is where the sun shines brightest. Trees, vines and other plants compete with each other to capture light energy and turn it into useful chemical energy in the form of sugar. Around four-fifths of the food made by rainforest plants is produced here, in the treetops.

This insect, called a katydid, lives in the tops of trees.

Fruit treats

All of this plant growth means that there is plenty to eat in the canopy in the form of leaves, shoots, flowers and fruit. Many rainforest animals spend their entire lives feasting in the treetops and never go down to the forest floor.

Colourful birds, such as parrots, toucans and hummingbirds fly in the treetops. Climbing animals such as monkeys, frogs, squirrels and lizards are also found there in large numbers. Everywhere there are insects, in a dazzling variety of colour and shape found nowhere else in the world.

Yummy!
The fisherman bat lives in trees but swoops down over rivers to snatch up fish in its claws.

Fruit bat

Canopy bats

Bats are so common in rainforests that sometimes there can be more bats there than any other mammal. Many bats will eat fruit, or take nectar from flowers, which helps to pollinate the plant. Other bats eat a lot of insects. A single bat can eat 1,000 mosquitoes in just one hour.

Bats are also an important food source for other animals along the food chain. Boa constrictors are very fond of eating bats and will dart out to ambush them. Owls, like bats, are night-time fliers and they will also catch bats.

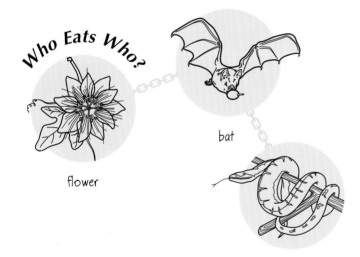

Who Eats Who?

flower

bat

boa

Don't eat me!

Many rainforest insects have incredible camouflage to hide them from the eyes of predators. There are insects that look like twigs, bark, flower parts, dead leaves, living leaves and even half-eaten leaves.

The leaf-imitating katydid mimics a living green leaf.

Food rewards

Sometimes it seems that plants actually want to be eaten. They produce brightly coloured flowers and sweet, fragrant fruits to attract insects and other animals. Of course, there is a good reason for this.

The birds and the bees

Plants, like any other living thing, need to reproduce to make more plants, just like themselves. But being rooted to the spot, a plant can't travel around and find a mate in the way an animal can. So, plants use other creatures to help them out.

For a new plant to grow from seed, pollen has to be taken from one flower to another in a process known as pollination. When bees and birds visit a flower for sweet, energy-rich pollen and nectar, some of the plant pollen sticks to the bee or bird and is carried by them to the next flower they visit.

Yummy!

Strangler fig fruits are eaten by rainforest animals who then leave fig seeds around the treetops in their droppings. When the seed germinates, it grows a long root all the way down to the forest floor.

South American howler monkeys love eating fruit.

Seed dispersal

Rainforest monkeys, such as spider monkeys, swing effortlessly from branch to branch in the canopy, gathering fruit and nuts. They consume a huge amount of fruit and many of the seeds they eat pass straight through and out the other end of the monkey unharmed. Safely wrapped in a package of fertilizer in the form of a monkey dropping, the seeds fall to the ground where they germinate, take root and grow.

A hummingbird in flight approaches a flower in order to drink the nectar inside.

Yummy!

Hummingbirds' tongues have barbs to hook insects out of flowers.

Hummingbirds and hunters

Hummingbirds are agile fliers and love the sweet nectar produced by rainforest flowers. Often hummingbirds are part of a very short food chain made up of just the bird and its food plant. But certain birds of prey in the rainforest specialize in catching hummingbirds. A hummingbird can find itself in a slightly longer chain that includes a flower, a fruit fly, a hummingbird and a hawk.

Life in miniature

A large habitat, such as the rainforest, holds a number of smaller habitats within it. Some are as small as a pool of water trapped by the leaves of a plant. And there are food chains here, too.

At home on the trees

Some rainforest plants are not rooted in the ground but are anchored to tree trunks and branches. But these plants do not feed off the tree. Like other plants, they capture the energy of sunlight in order to survive and grow. All they need is a place to live in the sun!

Many rainforest plants grow high in the trees.

Tree ponds

Bromeliads grow on rainforest trees in South America. They have no roots and take in minerals from rainwater through special hairs in their thick waterproof leaves, which grow in a circle around the stalk. The rainwater collects in the middle, forming a miniature pond that becomes home to a number of tiny rainforest dwellers.

A bromeliad pond provides minibeasts with water to drink and plant debris on which to feed.

Help from the desert

Bromeliads growing on trees on the east coast of Brazil get their minerals from a remarkable source. They are carried on the wind across the Atlantic Ocean from sandstorms in the Sahara Desert.

Pool chains

Over 250 different types of animal have been found living in bromeliad ponds. They are home to insect larvae, which hatch and grow in the ponds, where they feed on bits of leaf and other plant matter that fall into the pool. In turn, they are eaten by other insect larvae, frogs and their tadpoles. Fierce dragonfly nymphs sometimes eat the tadpoles.

Who Eats Who?

Decaying leaves and other plant debris in bromeliad pond

insect larvae

tadpole

dragonfly nymph

monkey

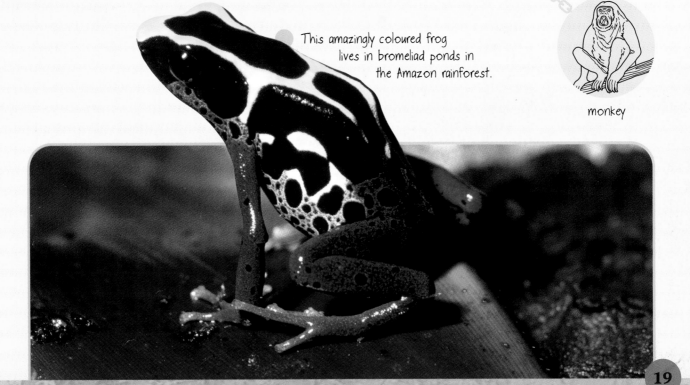

This amazingly coloured frog lives in bromeliad ponds in the Amazon rainforest.

Up and down the trees

Many animals of the rainforest are expert climbers, so they can spend time at different levels in the forest.

Night foragers

Big-eyed bushbabies leap fearlessly from branch to branch in the night-time forests of Africa. Usually they forage high in the treetops, catching insects and eating fruit.

Sometimes, though, a bushbaby might be tempted to come down to the ground in search of a mouse or eggs from a bird's nest. However, a bushbaby isn't quite as agile on the ground as it is in the trees. A sharp-eyed owl can suddenly swoop down and snatch up the bushbaby in its sharp claws.

Bushbaby

Who Eats Who?

seeds

rodent

bushbaby

owl

Ant farms

Leafcutter ants are unusual among insects because they grow their own food. Parties of leafcutters march out of their underground nests in the forest floor and climb up the tree trunks. Using their sharp jaws they cut up plant leaves and carry the pieces back down the tree to their nest.

Here they chew the leaves into a pulp, mixing them with saliva. A fungus grows on the chewed-up leaves, which the ants collect and eat. The fungus, not the plant leaves, is the ants' only source of food. So the ants are secondary consumers, and not primary consumers as they might at first appear to be.

Ant snacks

The hard-working leafcutter ants don't escape attention in the rainforest. The giant anteater can easily follow the parade of ants back down to their nest. Ripping open the nest with its powerful claws, it scoops up the helpless ants with its long sticky tongue.

Yummy!

A leafcutter ant can carry a piece of leaf that weighs 50 times more than the ant itself does.

A working party of leafcutter ants

Life on the ground floor

As mentioned earlier, most rainforest life exists in the treetops. Little light reaches the ground below so few plants can grow there. This means there is not much food for ground-dwelling animals to eat.

Hunters and collectors

Certain small-sized animals do survive on the rainforest floor by feeding on fruit and seeds that fall from the branches above.

In South American rainforests live cat-sized rodents, called agoutis. An agouti has to be alert as it searches for food. Jaguars prowling through the forest will catch and eat agoutis, and so will the racoon-like coatis.

Agoutis forage for fruit and seeds. Often they bury seeds to eat later. But sometimes the seeds never get eaten and germinate to grow into new trees.

Adaptable antelopes

Several different kinds of antelopes, called duikers, are found in African rainforests. Each kind has adapted to a particular diet of fruit and nuts. One duiker has a flexible jaw that allows it to eat large pieces of fruit. The main predators of duikers include leopards and pythons.

Agoutis forage on the rainforest floor in South America.

Pig in the wood

Wild pigs, or peccaries, roam the rainforests rooting around for roots, fruits, insects and other small animals. With their wide, varied diet these animals can occupy several different places on the food chain.

Wild pigs are fierce protectors of their territory and don't make easy prey. However, a large hunter, such as a big cat or snake, may still capture an unwary pig by surprise and eat it.

We're in the chain!

The Mbuti people of the Congo region in Africa live in the rainforest. They rely on birds to guide them across the forest floor to wild bees' nests, from which they gather honey to eat.

Wild pigs, or peccaries, eat many kinds of rainforest foods.

Who Eats Who?

fruit

duiker

leopard

Stuck in the middle

Animals in the middle of a food chain have two main food-related concerns. The first is to find enough food to eat. The second is to avoid being eaten.

Slow, slow, quick, quick, slow

Chameleons are a type of lizard found in the forests of Africa, where they hunt for insects in the trees and bushes. Chameleons move very, very slowly. This has two advantages. First, their insect prey are not aware of their approach, and second, the chameleon avoids attracting the attention of a larger predator.

Once the chameleon gets within striking distance of an insect it flicks out its long sticky tongue almost faster than a human eye can follow. The insect has little chance of escaping and any predator nearby has little chance of spotting the chameleon. After its meal the chameleon resumes its slow progress.

Yummy!

The three-toed sloth is another animal that relies on moving slowly to escape being seen. The slow sloth can take as long as a month to digest a meal of leaves.

Zap! A chameleon catches its dinner.

Colourful confusion

The chameleon has another advantage. It can change colour to blend in to its background. It turns green to match leaves, or brown to match bark. Other animals use camouflage too. The South American emerald boa can't change colour but its bright green coloration makes it hard to spot in the leafy rainforest. So, the boa can hunt its prey of birds and other small animals while avoiding being seen by the bigger eagles that would attack and eat it!

Killer spider

In the rainforests of South America a formidable predator prowls the forest floor. With a legspan of some 25 centimetres, you would not want to find a bird-eating spider in your bath! Bird-eating spiders hunt insects, lizards and frogs. They will also snatch baby birds from their nests, which is how they get their name. However, bigger animals, such as coatis – a kind of large rodent – will dig into the spider's burrow for an eight-legged snack!

Emerald boa

Who Eats Who?

flower

insect

frog

coati

spider

Kings of the jungle

At the top of the food chain are the super-predators, the big hunters of the forest. There are never very many large hunters because a lot of energy has been lost this far along the chain and there isn't much room at the top of the food pyramid. However, these rainforest hunters are among the most skilled predators in the world.

Top cats

Cats are the biggest hunters prowling the rainforest. In Asia there is the tiger, in South America the jaguar and in Africa the leopard. All of these big cats are formidable hunters. Large animals, such as pigs, are often hard to find in the rainforest so the cats have adapted to eat smaller ones. The jaguar, for example, is an excellent swimmer and skilled at catching fish. It will also eat frogs and turtles.

The rainforest is also home to smaller cats such as the margay and ocelot of South America and the leopard cat of Asia. These animals are generally not much bigger than a pet cat or small dog. Most of these smaller cats hunt at night. They are agile and lightweight enough to hunt their prey both on the forest floor and up in the canopy.

Aerial attackers

Eagles are big, fearsome predators. The harpy eagles of South America and the monkey-eating eagles of the Philippines are over a metre long with two-metre wingspans.

When an eagle spots its prey it dives low down into the trees and then swoops up again to attack the unsuspecting victim from below. These fast, powerful birds can snatch up small pigs, squirrels and lemurs. The harpy eagle also preys on slow-moving sloths.

Monkey-eating eagle

Who Eats Who?

leaves

harpy eagle

sloth

Yummy!

"Jaguar" comes from a Native American word meaning "killer that takes its prey in a single bound".

A black jaguar, also known as a black panther

Food web

sloth

Here is a food web that could be found in a South American rainforest. Surrounding it are some fascinating rainforest facts.

toucan

Nearly one-third of the total weight of plants in the world grows in the rainforests.

leaves
fruit
flowers

The slow-moving sloth is a habitat all by itself. Hundreds of beetles live in its fur, feeding on the algae that grows there.

frog

insect

Some scientists believe that there could be 50 million different kinds of insects and other minibeasts living in the rainforests.

Up to 900 centimetres of rain can fall on the rainforest in a year — six times more than in the wettest parts of Britain.

The Brazil nut tree produces tough fruits the size of cannon balls. Each fruit contains up to 20 hard-shelled nuts. The trees rely largely on sharp-toothed agoutis for seed dispersal.

owl

The tallest trees in the rainforest can reach 40 metres high.

harpy eagle

bat

jaguar

Each of the world's 900 or so different kinds of fig tree is only pollinated by its own particular kind of fig wasp.

snake

bird

Cecropia trees have special structures under their leaf stems that provide food for fierce Azteca ants. In return, the ants will swiftly attack any other animal that tries to eat the cecropia.

Glossary

adapted

suited to life in a particular environment.

camouflage

markings, shape or colour of an animal that make it difficult to see.

canopy

the "roof" of the rainforest; the topmost part of the forest trees.

consumer

an organism that eats another living thing to get energy; primary consumers eat plants; secondary consumers eat animals.

decomposers

organisms that break down the remains of dead plants and animals.

fertile

able to support growth.

food chain

the feeding links between living things, a guide to who eats whom.

food web

a map of all the feeding links in a habitat showing how plants and animals are connected to each other.

forage

to search for something to eat.

germinate

to start to grow; a seed produces its first roots and shoots when it germinates.

habitat

the place where a living thing makes its home.

herbivore

an animal that eats plants.

larvae

the young form of some insects, such as mosquitoes, that look quite different to the adults.

mammal

a warm-blooded animal with fur or hair, such as a leopard or a human. Female mammals produce milk to feed their young.

nutrients

another word for food; nutrients are all the things needed for a balanced diet.

nymph

the young form of some insects, such as dragonflies, that look similar to the adults.

organism

a living thing.

photosynthesis

the process by which plants capture
the energy of sunlight to make sugar.

pollinated

when grains of pollen are carried from one
flower to another; when this has happened
seeds can begin to form.

predator

an animal that catches and eats other
animals; predators are also called
carnivores.

prey

animals that are caught and eaten
by predators.

producer

an organism that makes, or produces, its own
food; producers are the source of
energy for the rest of the food chain.

recycling

reusing waste materials.

Rainforest Websites

http://www.rainforestheroes.com/kidscorner/
Be a hero – help protect the rainforest.

http://rainforest.image-centre.com/trees.html
A simple guide to the layers of a rainforest.

http://www.howstuffworks.com/rainforest.htm/
Lots of good clear information about rainforests and how they work.

http://www.cloudforestalive.org/library/sounds.f1ml
Sounds of the rainforest to download and listen to!

http://yahooligans.yahoo.com/science_and_nature/the_earth/ecology/rainforests/
A directory of rainforest links – ready to click!

Index